This book belongs to
_____

Ella Fitzgerald

By Mary Nhin

This book is dedicated to my children - Mikey, Kobe, and Jojo.

Copyright © 2023 by Grow Grit Press LLC. All rights reserved. No part of this book may be reproduced in any form without permission in writing from the publisher. Please send bulk order requests to growgritpress@gmail.com Printed and bound in the USA. MiniMovers.tv
Paperback ISBN: 978-1-63731-688-7 Hardcover ISBN: 978-1-63731-690-0

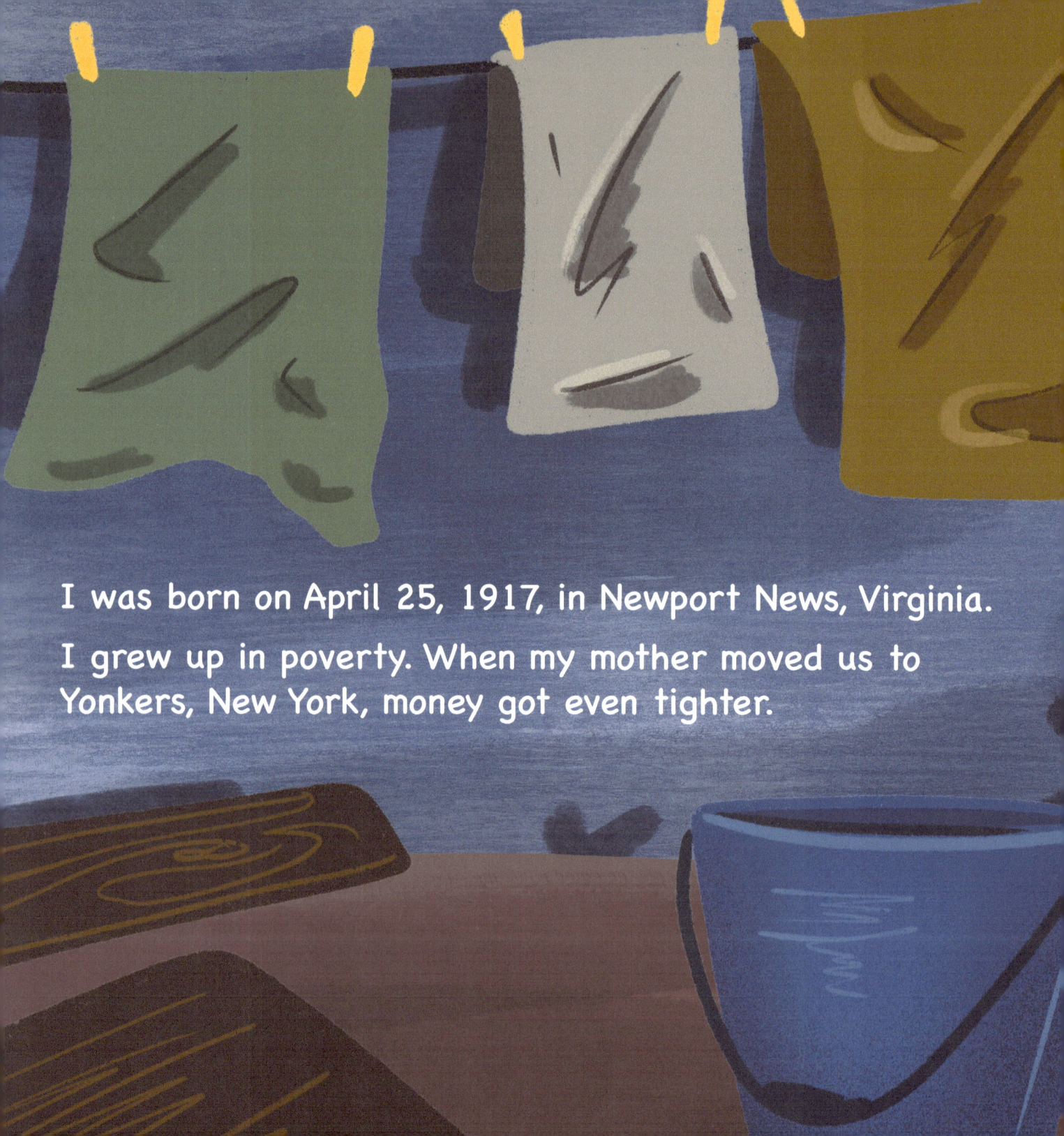

I was born on April 25, 1917, in Newport News, Virginia.

I grew up in poverty. When my mother moved us to Yonkers, New York, money got even tighter.

I helped out by taking small jobs like delivering groceries and running errands.

Even though times were hard, I found a way to stay positive. One thing that helped me a lot was music. Oftentimes, I pretended I was a singer on the radio.

One day, my mom brought home some records and I fell in love with Boswell Sisters' lead singer, Connie Boswell. I tried so hard to sound like her!

Those records inspired me to follow my dream of becoming a famous singer!

When I turned 15, my mom passed away from a car accident. I had to live with my stepfather. He wasn't a kind man.

I was able to get away from him and went to a New York training school for girls.

I never gave up on my dream, though. I would sing on the streets of Harlem in hopes of having my voice heard!

When I turned 17, I signed up for a talent contest at the Apollo Theater in Harlem.

I was so nervous!

I sang the song called "Judy" and I won first place! I was so happy and my singing career began to grow.

The very next year, I performed in the Tiny Bradshaw band at the Harlem Opera house.

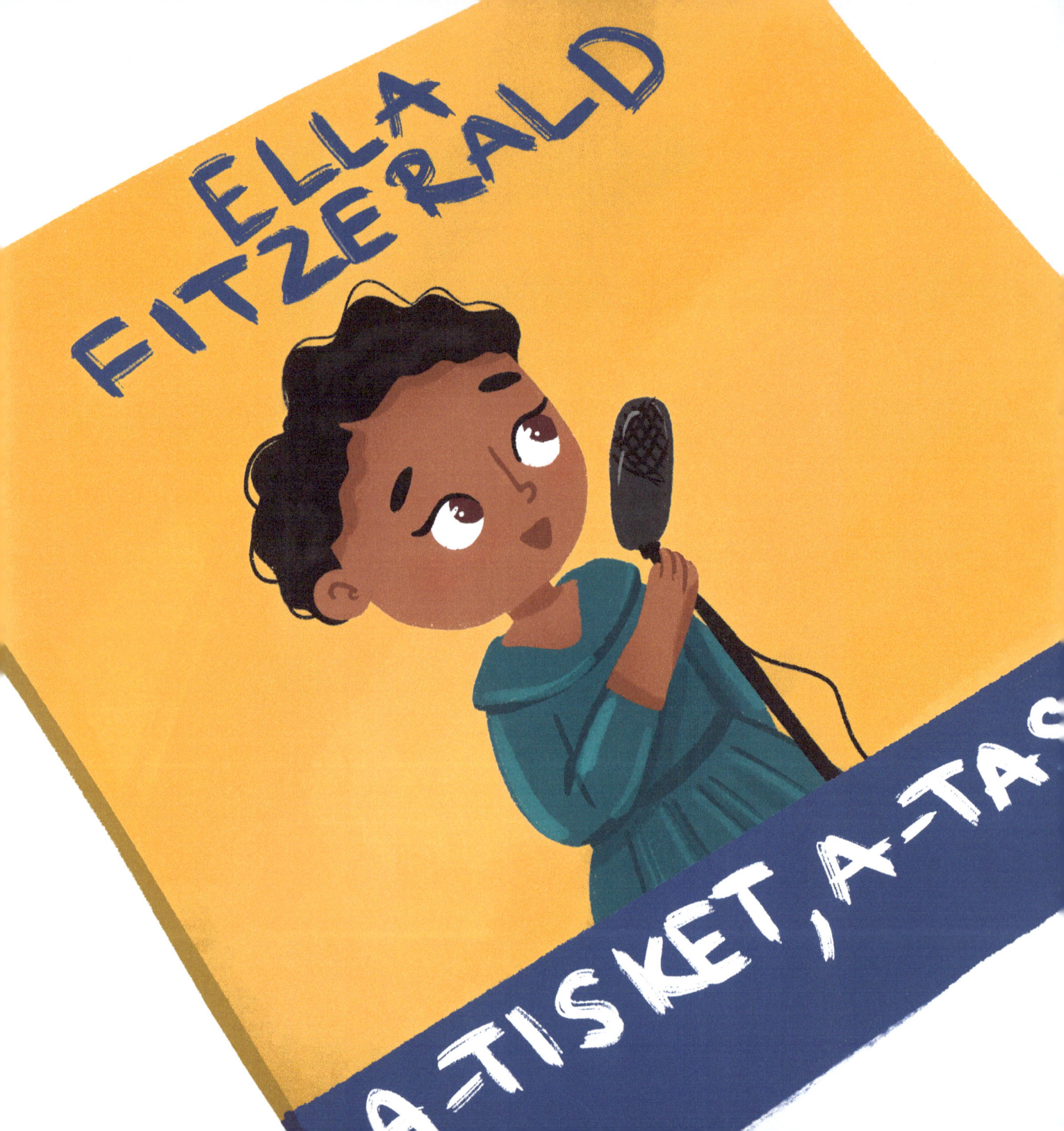

After being approved at the audition, I performed in the Chick Webb Orchestra.

I released a few songs after this, but the song called "A-Tisket, A-Tasket" was my major hit. It was the biggest hit record in a decade!

I sang the song called "Judy" and I won first place! I was so happy and my singing career began to grow.

The very next year, I performed in the Tiny Bradshaw band at the Harlem Opera house.

I later joined Benny Goodman Orchestra and faced many racial discriminations. It wasn't common for black and white performers to work together in the same band.

Benny Goodman believed in racial integration, and I was picked based on my performance.

It was difficult because there were still some buildings I couldn't go into because of my color, but my bandmates could because they were white.

Even so, we paved the way showing that white and blacks can work together and inspired others to do the same.

My audience was diverse too. They were rich and poor, made up of all races, all religions and all nationalities.

In my life, I won 13 Grammy awards, the Lifetime Achievement Award, and sold over 40 million albums. I was able to make my dreams come true with grit and passion!

Just don't give up trying to do what you really want to do. Where there is love and inspiration, I don't think you can go wrong.

Timeline

1934 - Ella wins amateur night at the Apollo

1935 - Ella joins Chick and Webb Orchestra

1938 - "A-Tisket, A-Tasket" becomes Ella's first hit song

1939 - Ella begins recording with the Benny Goodman Orchestra

1967 - Ella wins Lifetime Achievement Award

1987 - Ella is awarded National Medal of Art

minimovers.tv

 @marynhin   @officialninjalifehacks
#minimoversandshakers

 Ninja Life Hacks

Mary Nhin   Ninja Life Hacks

 @officialninjalifehacks

www.ingramcontent.com/pod-product-compliance
Lightning Source LLC
Chambersburg PA
CBHW041522070526
44585CB00002B/51